About the Author

Paul Geoffrey Belz is a writer and a science and nature educator who loves to explore the mountains, streams, and forests near Chico, California, where he lives with his partner Kate Roark. His poetry and prose appear in a range of magazines and anthologies, and on several websites. His many passions include international travel and adventures in the United States, vegetarian cooking, a range of books and films, and creative work with kids. He also loves long walks around Pittsburgh, Pennsylvania, his original hometown.

His book about the human and natural history of Chico, California's Bidwell Park is scheduled for publication later this year.

Sometimes the Soul Needs Chocolate:

Pandemic Odes

Paul Belz

Sometimes the Soul Needs Chocolate:

Pandemic Odes

Vanguard Press

VANGUARD PAPERBACK

© Copyright 2023
Paul Belz

The right of Paul Belz to be identified as author of this work has been asserted by him in accordance with the Copyright, Designs and Patents Act 1988.

All Rights Reserved

No reproduction, copy or transmission of this publication may be made without written permission.
No paragraph of this publication may be reproduced, copied or transmitted save with the written permission of the publisher, or in accordance with the provisions of the Copyright Act 1956 (as amended).

Any person who commits any unauthorised act in relation to this publication may be liable to criminal prosecution and civil claims for damages.

A CIP catalogue record for this title is available from the British Library.

ISBN 978 1 80016 989 0

*Vanguard Press is an imprint of
Pegasus Elliot Mackenzie Publishers Ltd.*
www.pegasuspublishers.com

First Published in 2023

**Vanguard Press
Sheraton House Castle Park
Cambridge England**

Printed & Bound in Great Britain

For Kate. We've been together through all this and far, far more!

Many people provided feedback and support as I wrote and developed this book. Special thanks go to Ralph Dranow, Norm Milstein, Kate Clark, Linda Champanier, Jean Varda, Linda Serrato, Sandy Makau, Bob Garner, Marcus Colasurdo, David Aust, Jeanette Keables, Doug Aiken, Jennifer Bransky, Lucille Lang Day, Genevieve Smith, Joan Goodreau and especially Kate Roark.

Contents

ODE TO A PENCIL	13
ODE TO FEELING FED UP	14
ODE TO CONFINED REDWOODS	16
ODE TO HATING A FREEWAY	17
ODE TO BIG CHICO CREEK	18
ODE TO A CANADA GOOSE	20
ODE TO BUMPASS HELL	22
ODE TO THE WIND	23
ODE TO A FEATHER	24
ODE TO CAMPING	25
ELECTION 2020 ODE	27
PLANETARY CONJUNCTION ODE	29
ODE TO NEEDING POETS	31
ODE TO SOCIAL CHANGE	33
ODE TO CHOCOLATE	34
ODE TO A SQUIRREL	35
HOME TOWN ODE	36
ODE TO BEETHOVEN	38
ODE TO LIPTON TEA	40
ODE TO ODDNESS	42
ODE TO IGNORING A JOB AD	44
ODE TO MASKS	46
ODE TO SECOND VACCINE	47
ODE TO THE PANDEMIC'S END	48

ODE TO A PENCIL

Hey, wand! Make me a wizard!
Let me howl to hidden words,
call them from my brain tissue, hormones, blood.
Make them flash down my spine, charge through my arm,
hand, and fingers, into you.
Do you tremble when these sparks
gather at your paper-scratching tip,
tingle as we fill notebooks with song,
wear yourself out with this frenzied work,
then shout through my arm to my heart and skull,
beg for more images, off-rhymes, beats
you can place in a new-born poem?
Let my deluge of words be a cycle
like clouds that chill into rain,
fall to play the bongo drum earth,
drench soil, then flow through roots,
up stems, back to leaves, change to steam,
gather to form healing raindrops once more.
Pencil, may my verses be spells and storms.

ODE TO FEELING FED UP

Enough!
We're done with growing weary from doing nothing,
squishing our butts into the couch,
dozing off during innocuous TV.
Enough!
We're sick of meeting on-line,
seeing people become blips on screens.
They change colors, turn upside down.
Their voices become feedback. No one can hug.
Enough!
We want to share chocolate cake,
chips and guac, pumpkin pie, pinot noir.
Enough of being forced into small rooms!
The forest still demands that we come.
It greets us with gold and crimson leaves.
Sandhill cranes migrate overhead,
call to us with a glockenspiel's tones:
"You're safe here if you hike alone,
or with your lonesome loved one.
Tell your sadness to hawks,
red mushrooms, acorns, deer, us." Thanks, birds!
We're done with liars who say, "All's well!"

Yeah! Worn down by multiple deaths,
sick of growing numbness that feeds on exhaustion,
we cry, "Enough!"

ODE TO CONFINED REDWOODS

I want to be your jailbreak friend
who'll lift your roots from parched soil.
We'll sneak away from this parking lot
where you're confined. The coast calls us. Its summer fog
is your true water. Here, where you're caged,
a sprinkler turns dry earth around you damp,
not soaked. Scrub jays and red-shouldered hawks
perch on your branches. You like them fine,
but yearn for spotted owls
and marbled murrelets to nest on you.
Thirsty pets, you stand here in straight rows,
shade parked cars in this summer-drenched land.
I'll free you all! We'll hide by day,
hunker down in warehouses and barns,
follow shooting stars by night,
sneak across freeways, drink from creeks
until we get to your fog-nurtured home
just past the salty sea wind's reach.
Let's run to the Pacific!
Sorry. Damn!
I can't find the key to your cage. We're stuck.
You greet me like chained dogs when I step outside.
Teach me to bark.

ODE TO HATING A FREEWAY

You hiss, unlike a snake who feeds on rats,
glistens as it basks, blends with sand and stones,
skedaddles when people approach,
and almost never says "Sssssss."
You rumble, more weakly than the tempest sea
who knows how to deepen its tones,
draw them out like a conch shell's sighs.
You cry out, unlike the circling hawk
whose voice, a flute that bounces from grassy hills,
plays a descending scale.
You tremble, but don't mimic thunder's moans.
No, you bang, shriek, crack like a falling oak
or a shattered stained-glass window,
constant motion, with no pattern.
Drivers race, honk, curse, ignore the world.
Casinos, fast food, gas, malls are what they seek.
Everything else blurs. Demon, I'll drive you out.

ODE TO BIG CHICO CREEK

Rambler who runs to the Pacific,
gypsy caravan made from water,
you slither and sing past pipevine and red bud
while sunlight pirouettes on rocks.
Tell me whose bodies once clutched you.
T. rex! Your particles flashed through its legs
as it faced triceratops' horns
or dashed after clever trachodon.
Other molecules streamed skyward through oaks' roots,
then waited for the sun to yank them up
to chilled air, where they gathered as clouds.
They tumbled onto roses, mallards, pines.
Rain landed on people. Did some drench Darwin,
who strolled on the *Beagle*'s deck and watched spiders
cling to bits of webs and ride the wind
over the sea, onto his nose?
Some of your molecules sat inside Marx,
who smoked and wrote about commodities.
Frida Kahlo held water in her eyes
and studied the colors of her paint.
Rachel Carson found your molecules on her beach,
where she showed her young nephew ghost crabs.

Water fled from these folks as sweat,
water vapor in their breath, and pee.
It made its way to mountains' slopes,
then fell as snow to melt and renew you, creek.
New drops ramble over sandstone and mud.
Salmon seize your molecules, yield them to bears.
Sycamore roots yank more inside.
Many rise to the beckoning sun
or fly away on an osprey's beak
after it grabs a fish and gets soaked.
Some particles reach the ocean,
spend years as waves, tides,
octopuses' homes. I watch you slide by,
while heat takes water from my skin.
I'm parched. If I drink from you,
I'll take in multitudes.

ODE TO A CANADA GOOSE

You waddle over ebony basalt,
pass purple lupines, orange poppies
that fill cracks in volcanic rock
that's so rugged any walker might slip—
coyote, deer, human, bear. Wobble along.
You're not built for land, tan-breasted one.
How do you fare so well here,
stunned by life in the hot dust,
so close to the crackling stream
where you can paddle, swim, and thrive?
Did hunger or wonder bring you?

Maybe your black eyes revel in grass
that's so emerald it nearly stings.
Grazing bird who plucks algae from ponds,
do unknown blossoms taste good—
lemon buttercups, cherry-red columbines?
You could grasp them in your beak,
swallow them in bits, but you don't eat.
Can you revel and dream of more than food,
take notes on the chemistry of sweet scents,
hot colors, satin textures, round or diamond leaves?

Do you create poems — dialogues with flowers?
Ignorant humans need to know your mind.
Translate "Roonk!" for us.

ODE TO BUMPASS HELL

I find myself in a yellow place.
A few pines grow on dusty slopes
where rocks and soil are butterscotch bright.
Everything smells like sulfur, and I'm safe,
high in these explosive mountains,
far enough from cursed wildfires,
forests and towns turned to ash.
The sky above is spotless, pure,
here where boulders rumble.
Magma-heated steam hisses, smashes
through volcanic rock and rises
towards blue skies like a singing breath.
This chaotic beauty, this peaceful home
cries "Havoc! Nightmares be gone!"
I'm protected. Some claim demons howl here;
I don't find them in this sanctuary.
High slopes shelter us from fires.
I'm safe here. Sulfur sure smells good!

Lassen Volcanic National Park, October 2020

ODE TO THE WIND

Jitterbug dancer who spins the dust,
parched thief who steals water from leaves:
pines and oaks sing to you, pollen bearer!
Once you licked my skin, wrapped around my spine,
tugged me from my flesh. I became you!
We flew upslope towards mountains' rocky crowns.
I was water vapor, tumbling nitrogen,
gasses I couldn't name or count.
We streaked for the clouds, and you set me down,
back in my body that I'd never left.
You caressed my forehead. I breathed you in,
stunned and solid as a birch.
The world flowed through me. I forgot my name.

ODE TO A FEATHER

You're a raincoat. Water beads up
and slides away. Birds don't mind storms—
you keep them warm in chilled wind.
You're their umbrella; they never leave you at home.
You hold countless colors — natural make-up
no one needs to buy. The bright and loud get dates;
the quiet know how to sneak around.
You scoop rushing air and lift hawks,
snow geese, pelicans, cranes.
Storks fly so high they disappear.
Some used to claim they reached the moon, spent winter
    there.
You help owls fly silently when they hunt.
T. rex and deinonychus held you close,
used you for their soft clothes.
People changed you into quill pens.
If I find one, I'll write like a bird!

ODE TO CAMPING

I wake in a bird song world.
Black-headed grosbeak's "Twitter!", raven's "Aawnk!",
pileated woodpecker's "Thud! Thud! Thud!"
all throw echoes around these firs.

Meanwhile, the nation broils,
set on fire by a knee
that crushed a man's breath.

Morning sky turns from gray to tan,
pink, then soft blue. Copper-colored Mars
fades, followed by the crescent moon.

Hospitals turn the dying away.
They stumble along sidewalks,
beg for a crack in the door.

Warmth flows from the growing day,
chased away by the night's cool wind.
Orange butterflies ride the breeze,
fly in zig-zag paths, look drunk
as they dodge hungry birds.

Chipmunk scans the waking world.
Peace lifts me from repeating thoughts
whose blankness follows despair.
Can I briefly claim the right to be sane?
I walk with red and gold blossoms,
and blue mayflies that live for a day.

Thoughts of devastated people snatch me.
They ache from evictions and debts.
Hunger and thirst are their breakfast.
Their eyes seize me as I rejoice,
demand, "What do you have for us?"
I stop my dance, make myself still,
say, "I give you this cedar's incense.
Can it help?"

ELECTION 2020 ODE

Out on my deck with a glass of sauvignon,
I feel November's cool wind,
watch high cirrus clouds scratch the sky,
while ravens' "Aawks!" follow them.

Once in a while, things are all right,
even good. Maybe we'll learn to think again,
wrangle and argue without curses,
semi-automatics or flames.
Maybe we can walk like inchworms,
undeterred as we slither through rubbish piles
towards ravens, the moon, and dusk.
So many times, we rang with hope,
believed in resurrection, hoped that death,
gloom, exploitation cracked into shards
as we slashed our ways out from cells
and flew towards dawn. So many times
we found ourselves snatched, driven
down to hot tar, dust, sludge,
the sick past's attacks. Here we are,
just outside of the shattered tomb
that could still yank us, howling, back.

The other night I saw a shooting star
illuminate November's sky,
whisper through autumn's night.
Let it give us strength.

November 7, 2020

PLANETARY CONJUNCTION ODE

Distanced, masked, scared, we stood in dry grass,
watched the sun sneak behind western peaks.
It pulled the colors orange, yellow, pink behind
so our hillside could turn dark.
Quarter moon appeared in cream-colored sky.
We thought of ventilators, dry coughs,
fevers, and waited for two planets to appear.
No evil stalked us through the dark.
This was shooting star's night.
Nebulae, galaxies, solar wind, star clusters
came together. This was owls' time.
They filled the night with cries and whooooos,
prelude to mating. Deer wandered through shadows.
Chrysalises clung to oaks, sheltered larvae.
This was dusk, the hour of birth;
Solstice, the night that sings to dawn.
Terrors clung to our flesh and hugged us tight:
loss of the senses taste and smell,
hospitals without any beds,
governors' requests for body bags.
Shivering, we scanned the sky
for two planets, called them to make us burn

as the air grew chilled. We ignored the blazing clouds,
the faithful moon, and the messengers came,
entered the sky without a blast or shout.
Jupiter, bright lightning that lacked thunder,
hazy Saturn, that moment after a dream —
both stuck around, refused to fade,
candles that called us into winter's night.
We thought they were close enough to high-five,
share a joke, flirt, make out. Really, millions of miles
filled with dark matter, zipping photons,
scattered atoms lay between. This was OK.
We saw them as a spark, a steady chant,
a call. Now we remembered
moon, fading sunlight, stars that blinked in.
We let the sky eat our fear.

December 21, 2020

ODE TO NEEDING POETS

Hey Despair, we're breaking up! You're not my love,
even when you cuddle me close,
watch me with cracked yellow eyes, whisper soft lies—
"Let me numb you. These aren't poets' days.
They'll shred you with feelings and false dreams.
Let me comfort you with hopeless peace." No!
I leap out of your empty bed. Bye-bye!
I dash out of your sludge-filled house,
find my car. My escape will be rough,
I grumble as I drive. Yes, you shadow me.
We skid down sleet-covered roads at three a.m.
Poets start to ring in my mind.
They whisper blazing words that try to burn
trash you dumped in me. You muffle them.
I can barely hear. Who are these longtime friends
who call to me? Whitman? Dickinson? Neruda?
Harjo? Maybe Norm and Jean, who I know?
They come to fuel me and slash your tires
so I can jet away. You garble my heart.
If it were my radio, static would clog it.
Who would sing to me? Kate Wolf? John Prine?
I couldn't hear them as I sped through dark downs.

It's the same with these poets. Your tires shriek,
they blur my memory. I hit the gas.
Silent cars zip past, faster than me.
Drivers' radios are off, they cram their minds
with distractions and gloom to forget you.
Some dream of wrestling matches, porn,
movies filled with explosions and screams.
Others search off-ramps for open bars and grills
that serve pre-dawn burgers, onion rings,
tequila. Nothing frees them. You take charge.
Look, though. The next town's lights
shine behind snow-covered hills.
Poets live there. Their voices grow strong
in my weary mind. Williams. Levertov. Hass.
Sandy and Bob, who I've heard read at cafés.
Poems shove, and you fall behind.
I gasp and find a street I know,
a house with an unlocked door.
A couch has blankets, I hide from you.
Sleep fills me with verses. When I wake,
I'll feed my poet hosts with apples and tea.
Then we'll search for drivers who are stranded and lost.

ODE TO SOCIAL CHANGE

In a time of shouts, I whisper.
In a time of sandpaper and buzzsaws,
I make a stab at song.
I hide books in a bonfire time.
They cower together in my shadowed room,
where I bring them bread, soup, and wine.
I give them candle-lit tables and chairs;
they can argue, wrestle, dream.
In a demon time, I celebrate hope,
faith in bittersweet life,
knowing that all answers are flawed.
We can turn corners without stumbling.
In a time of gloom, I laugh.

ODE TO CHOCOLATE

You've got to linger with dark chocolate.
It's a waste if you chomp on it real fast,
thrust it to the back of your mouth,
swirl it with spit, squeeze it down your throat.
Then it will feel like melted wax,
taste kind of like sugar,
and "Gulp!" Nothing more. You'll think, "Huh?
What was that?" and walk away shrugging.
No. Concentrate. Bite little pieces thoughtfully.
Swish them. You might notice cinnamon,
nutmeg, vanilla beans, pepper—
sweet thunderstorms on your tongue.
Sometimes the soul needs chocolate
when we're flung towards chaos, and plagues.
Bigots, wildfires, and powerful fools
leap our way. Cacao lifts us up,
unbinds our tongues, helps us stand
on the speeding ground. Food of the gods,
keep us wild!

ODE TO A SQUIRREL

Small one, you love that hole in the fence!
You think it saved you again! I came by
laden with a bag of dirty clothes,
laundry-bound. Away you zipped!
Your tail bent down, and you made it through that hole!
Hey, I'm no threat. Only my eyes will catch you.
I'll see your shale-brown fur,
shorter than newborn grass,
your dark fudge eyes, twitching nose,
straight-line dash to that hole.
You got away from me! Watch for the hawk,
frenzied dogs, and pickup trucks' tires.
I'm harmless. All I do is write.

HOME TOWN ODE

Pittsburgh's cardinals' red feathers blaze.
They perch in maples, call "Pretty! Pretty!"
Humid air chills. Lightning yells, "Find shelter!"
I sit by a café window, sip Earl Grey,
hear thunder flow down the Ohio,
watch the day turn bittersweet with rain.
Pittsburgh. I'll always come back to you.
I've wandered through Istanbul and Kathmandu,
heard imams in minarets chant to dusk,
seen temple-goers ring bells to wake Ganesh,
watched Parisians tango by the Seine,
thrived on Dublin's curry with Guinness stout,
but I love Pittsburgh's roughness.
I'll always return, cobblestone town.
My flesh and mind are made from you,
long-ago smoke-stack city, place of dirty snow,
whose steel mills are gone now. I want your dinosaurs,
my childhood pals to stomp through your museum,
and yell, "Hey, world, Pittsburgh's great!"
Yeah, I wander redwood forests' paths,
hug their wild fungi, kiss their fog.
I sleep on volcano's roots and welcome stars.

Still, I miss your rivers, once polluted, now clean,
home to egrets, herons and geese.
I'll always come home to visit your trolleys, polkas,
pierogis and bricks, my firefly-filled town.

ODE TO BEETHOVEN

Ludwig, dude, I remember your joy, screams,
moans, sighs, hysterical laughs, praise for trees,
birds, sun, rain. I sat at my piano,
age ten, made my fingers bring you to life.
Death surrounded me. Aged aunts,
cousins, uncles always fell.
I cringed, shrank from clawed hands
that reached for me from gray corners.
You became my shelter, my strength.

I was often a happy kid.
Me and my gang thrived on forest hikes,
swimming holes in creeks, hide and seek
under streetlights, baseball at dusk,
cheering the Pirates from bleachers.
We created tales where Hercules and Tarzan
rallied lions, elephants, zebras, giraffes,
joined us kids to attack those clawed hands
and drive them from our world.
When I was alone,
stalked by colorless shadows, with no friends
to fight gloom with laughter, I sang you.

My fingers skipped along shining keys:
"Moonlight Sonata", "Für Elise". I stalled,
stumbled, but you still built a shield
that blocked claws. Ecstatic warrior, we still dance.

ODE TO LIPTON TEA

It's my private time machine—
a sting, a vague and bitter jolt
close to my tonsils, along my mouth's roof,
shifts me back to cinnamon toast and tea,
my mom's remedy for everything.
A crocheted blanket warmed me
on *I Love Lucy* mornings, home from third grade
with fever, twisting stomach, cement in my head.
The Dick van Dyke Show was next,
and I liked the noon news better than math,
penmanship, or catechism. A nap came,
an afternoon reading Mowgli or Jim Hawkins,
and more of that blessed tea.
I skipped

    over years to a ramshackle house,
dancing trees painted on the living room wall,
where we rumpled dreamers watched the snow
careen past our window. We shared jelly and toast
at our table. I dipped my teabag
into scalding water. Pennsylvania's cold
in March. My friends added milk

to instant Maxwell House.
Billy Holiday sang to us, then Grace Slick.
We debated Trotsky, Proudhon,
De Beauvoir, Marge Piercy, Camus,
Gurdjieff, St. Theresa, Don Juan,
we sweater-clad young women and men,
prophets of social collapse.
I began my comments with a rush of hot tea,
then I leapt over years to today,
where I find a cup of Lipton. I prefer
resonant, spicy sencha, genmaicha, Earl Grey.
But this welcome jolt pulls my scattered years
into one.

ODE TO ODDNESS

We slept beside freeway onramps,
sheltered by tall weeds. We hid from cops all night,
hitched rides with farmers, religious cults,
drunk truck drivers who passed on the road's shoulder,
kind folks and angel dust heads.
We learned to drive at forty. We're the odd.
We rescue twirling bees in swimming pools,
catch indoor spiders in cups, free them on shrubs,
brake for butterflies and crows — we're the odd.
We tune out the Superbowl,
run from its monotonal buzz,
prefer Walt Whitman to a quarterback,
can't define a line of scrimmage — we're the odd.
We loved weird Spiderman—
science nerd gone super, but still bookish,
bullied like we were and forced to hide his strength,
running through shadows from everyone who blamed him.
We're the odd.
We love broccoli—
its green flowers taste like topsoil,
it's better than bacon, that sizzling flesh
that clogs people with salty fat—

we're the odd.
We thrive on loneliness,
find shelter in basalt canyons,
where orange poppies and blue lupines thrive
and dusk caresses our skin. We wail with stars.
We're the odd.
Our words have their own shapes
and colors, don't mix with jigsaw language
that everyone else understands.
We're one version of the odd.
But celebrate — you're weird, too!

ODE TO IGNORING A JOB AD

Pale sign on cemetery's back fence
calls, "Now hiring!" No details, like the wage,
benefits, duties — just two words
that make me hide behind a laugh.
Would my boss demand total discipline—
no motion, nothing that would disturb
ants, beetles, fungi, grass, daisies, worms?
"Employees, whose work is to be dead,
lie on your backs, let time leave you alone.
You'll need talent for this lack of heart and thought,
then no feeling in your lips, skin, even your groin."

I'm so glad I don't need this work.
I couldn't record birds and their songs
without my hearing and sight.
I'd be useless monitoring weather
if my mind were so gone.
Gardening would be tough with numb, still hands.
Hmmm. Could I be a travel writer
sending dispatches from the next world?
Intriguing, but so far no one's work has arrived,
presenting the afterlife in an email.

I'll find earth-bound adventures to describe.
So, bye-bye sign. You'll find folks with no choice.
They'll flock to you. For now, I'll run away.

ODE TO MASKS

Yeah, life savers, pandemic blocks,
go away now! You're no big deal, but take a nap.
I'll give you quiet spots in a drawer,
let you rest when there's no more work.
I'll honor the most unique ones: zipping hummingbird,
Beatles crossing Abbey Road, when John forgot his mask,
and rainbow brachiosauruses in a row.
I'll keep plain ones, too, when you all retire,
if that day ever comes.
You're no problem. You saved many lives,
but may this virus end. We'll forget its taste,
song, texture, smell, the fear it creates.
I don't hate you masks, covid's foes,
but let us see smiles, chins, noses, cheeks,
faces made whole. If that day comes,
we'll dance and lay you down.

ODE TO SECOND VACCINE

Later that day, our western sky turns pale,
becomes pumpkin-colored at dusk.
Cool air flows around my cheeks and nose.
I'm weary, walking slowly, but I call,
"Hi there, oaks whose leaves are yet to come."
I chirp back to the tiny bird
who zips above the parking lit. "Eenk!
Eenk!" I reply. That sludge wall inside me falls.
I climb out of my closed brain, let my chest tingle.
People still stay apart. OK. This will pass.
Maybe we'll dance to salsa, reggae, jazz
through streets fueled by food trucks
and a touch of laughing beer.
I'm tired tonight, after my shot.
My body builds strength. Welcome, weariness!

ODE TO THE PANDEMIC'S END

I'll share my apple strudel
made from Granny Smiths so tart
everyone's mouth and tongue will sing.
Teeth will crunch the walnuts and crust.
Brown sugar, raisins, allspice and cloves
will flow through the warm juice,
and we'll sit down at the fireplace table.
You might bring coconut pudding, walnut pie,
mango juice, guacamole, and chips,
brownies, popcorn, deviled eggs.
We'll sit silently, think of those who are gone,
let ourselves mourn. A conch shell's call
will spring out from us. In a while, we'll feast,
break oatmeal cookies, pass them around.
Before long we'll laugh. Let there be tambourines!
Panpipes! Irish harps! Guitars!
The call to dance! We'll shake the walls!

www.ingramcontent.com/pod-product-compliance
Lightning Source LLC
LaVergne TN
LVHW041551060526
838200LV00037B/1232